Our New Fish Tank

Learning to Estimate to the Nearest Ones, Tens, and Hundreds Places

Kathleen Collins

Math
for the
REAL World™

New York

Published in 2004, 2010 by The Rosen Publishing Group, Inc.
29 East 21st Street, New York, NY 10010

Revised Edition

Book Design: Michael Tsanis

Photo Credits: Cover © Francisco Cruz/SuperStock; all interior photos by Maura B. McConnell.

ISBN: 978-0-8239-8881-5
6-pack ISBN: 978-0-8239-7390-3

Manufactured in the United States of America

CPSIA Compliance Information: Batch #WR113170RC: For further information contact Rosen Publishing, New York, New York at 1-800-237-9932.

Contents

The New Fish Tank

My friends and I wanted to get a fish tank for our classroom. We decided to have a bake sale to raise the money. We asked our teacher how much money we needed to raise. She told us to **estimate** how much it might cost first. We went to the library and found a book about pet fish. We made a list of all the things we would need to buy. First we needed to buy a fish tank.

Sasha's family has a fish tank in their home. Sasha's mother said that the fish tank cost about $70.00. We decided to get a smaller size than the one she had. We estimated that a smaller one would cost about $50.00.

Estimating and Rounding

Gravel for 1 fish tank costs $5.99. We **rounded** that to the nearest dollar. Rounding lets us quickly estimate how much something will cost. To help us round to the nearest dollar, we need to look at the number to the right of the **decimal point**. This number is in the tenths place.

When the number in the tenths place is 0, 1, 2, 3, or 4, we round down to the nearest dollar, or ones place. When the number in the tenths place is 5, 6, 7, 8, or 9, we round up to the nearest dollar.

Since there is a 9 in the tenths place, $5.99 is rounded up to $6.00. Now our estimated total is $56.00.

fish tank

gravel

things to buy:

fish tank	$50.00
gravel	+ $ 6.00
estimated total	$56.00

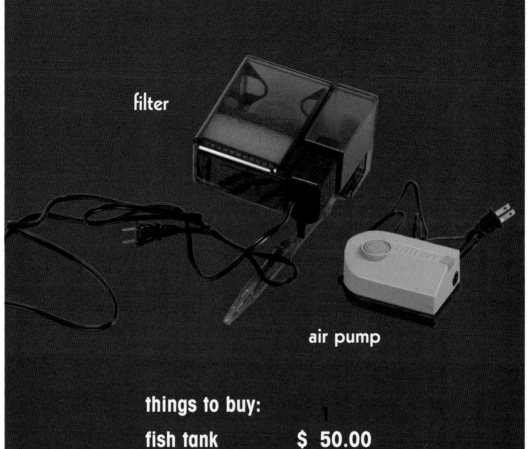

filter

air pump

things to buy:

fish tank	$ 50.00
gravel	$ 6.00
air pump	$ 10.00
filter	+ $ 26.00
estimated total	$ 92.00
	(that's about $90.00)

Pumps and Filters

A fish tank needs an **air pump** and a **filter**. We found an air pump that cost $9.59. We rounded that up to $10.00. We found a filter that cost $25.79. We rounded that up to $26.00.

Now our estimated total came to $92.00. We decided to round that number to the nearest tens place to make it easier to remember. Since the number in the ones place is 2, we rounded the total down to $90.00.

Altogether, the air pump and the filter would cost $35.38. If we rounded this number to the nearest tens place, would we round it to $40.00 or $30.00? We would round it to $40.00, because the number in the ones place is 5.

Help from the Pet Store Owner

We visited the pet store. We asked the owner about the things we would need for our fish tank. He told us the type of heater we needed for our tank would cost $16.99. We rounded that up to $17.00.

He also told us that we needed a **thermometer** so we could be sure the water didn't get too hot or too cold. The thermometer cost $3.69. We rounded that up to $4.00.

So far, our estimated total is $113.00. We can round that amount to the nearest tens place so it is easier to remember. Since the number in the ones place is 3, we round down to the nearest tens place. Now our estimated total is $110.00.

things to buy: 2

fish tank $ 50.00
gravel $ 6.00
air pump $ 10.00
filter $ 26.00
heater $ 17.00
thermometer   + $ 4.00
                  ─────────────
estimated total $113.00
                   (that's about $110.00)

heater

thermometer

2 goldfish

2 striped fish

estimate:	3	real cost:	44 5
fish tank	$ 50.00	fish tank	$ 50.00
gravel	$ 6.00	gravel	$ 5.99
air pump	$ 10.00	air pump	$ 9.59
filter	$ 26.00	filter	$ 25.79
heater	$ 17.00	heater	$ 16.99
thermometer	$ 4.00	thermometer	$ 3.69
fish	$ 16.00	fish	$ 16.38
food	+ $ 5.00	food	+ $ 5.45
estimated total	$134.00	total cost	$133.88
(that's about $130.00)			

Fish and Fish Food

We still needed the most important part of the fish tank—the fish! Two striped fish cost $13.00. Two goldfish cost $3.38. Altogether, the fish cost $16.38. We rounded that number down to $16.00. A box of fish food cost $5.45. We rounded that number down to $5.00. We added these costs to our estimated total. Our final estimated total came to $134.00.

We had our bake sale and raised $135.00! Finally, we bought our tank and supplies. The total came to $133.88. We were just $0.12 away from our estimated total!

Buying the Fish Tank

Our **principal** liked our fish tank very much. She decided that the other 4 classes should have bake sales so they could buy fish tanks, too. We told her that our fish tank cost $133.88 and that 4 fish tanks would cost $535.52. We rounded that number to the nearest hundreds place so it would be easier to remember. What number did we round it to? That's right, $535.52 rounded to the nearest hundreds place is $500.00!

Glossary

air pump (AYR PUHMP) A machine that forces air into the water of a fish tank.

decimal point (DEH-suh-muhl POYNT) A dot used in a number. In a dollar amount, the decimal point is between the dollars and cents.

estimate (EH-stih-mayt) To make a quick and careful guess about the amount, size, or value of something.

filter (FIL-tuhr) An instrument that keeps the water in a fish tank clean.

gravel (GRA-vuhl) Small pieces of rock and pebbles.

principal (PRIN-suh-puhl) The leader of a school.

round (ROWND) To change a number to the nearest ones place, tens place, hundreds place, and so on.

thermometer (thuhr-MAH-muh-tuhr) A tool that measures how hot or cold something is.

Index